POCKET ⌷ GUIDE

JOHN WESLEY'S

MESSAGE TODAY

LOVETT H. WEEMS, JR.

D1173450

ABINGDON PRESS
Nashville

For
Lovett Hayes Weems III
Cynthia Dee Weems
June Elizabeth Pittman Weems
Lawrence David Weems

POCKET GUIDE TO JOHN WESLEY'S MESSAGE TODAY

Copyright © 1982 assigned to Lovett H. Weems, Jr.
Abingdon Press edition 1991

This book is printed on acid-free paper.

Library of Congress Cataloging-in-Publications Data

Weems, Lovett Hayes.
    Pocket guide to John Wesley's message today / Lovett Hayes
Weems, Jr.—Abingdon Press ed.
        p.   cm.
    ISBN 0-687-31681-2 (alk. paper)
    1. Wesley, John, 1703-1791   1. Title.
BX8495.W5W42   1990
230'.7—dc20   90-21080

    94 95 96 97 98 99 00 01 02 — 11 10 9 8 7 6 5 4 3

MANUFACTURED IN THE UNITED STATES OF AMERICA

CONTENTS

PREFACE

Legend has it that a stranger visiting a community in England asked an old Cornishman to explain the obvious morality and spirit of the villagers. He replied, "A man named Wesley passed this way."

Divergent views still remain concerning Wesley and his historical and theological legacy, but no one can deny the impact of this man.

Stanley Ayling, a recent Wesley biographer whose understanding of the eighteenth century was previously demonstrated in his biographies of King George III and William Pitt, surveys Wesley's life with fairness and clarity. While Ayling avoids the often exaggerated estimates of Wesley by many Wesleyan bodies, this scholar declares Wesley to be "the single most influential Protestant leader of the English-speaking world since the Reformation."[1]

This book deals with the theological legacy of John Wesley. It seeks to locate those dominate themes which were at the heart of the preaching of Wesley and others who were a part of the Wesleyan Revival.

Thanks are in order to several persons. Albert C. Outler, whose guidance and encouragement I have appreciated since my student days at Perkins School of Theology, read the manuscript and helped with many historical and theological insights. Barbara

Brown, Assistant to the Dean at Candler School of Theology, also served as a reader and made numerous editorial and stylistic suggestions.

I appreciate the invitation of Jim L. Waits, Dean of Emory University's Candler School of Theology, to teach for a semester at Candler as Minister-in-Residence. Much of the research and writing of this work was done during that period.

Special thanks go to my secretary of many years, Rhonda Thomas, for her dedication, untiring work, and professional skill.

LOVETT H. WEEMS, JR.

INTRODUCTION

THEOLOGY AT THE HEART OF THE WESLEYAN REVIVAL

A number of years ago *Life* magazine stated in an article, "Methodism is long on organization and short on theology." In the same article reference was made to Methodism's "casual approach to theology."[1] This popular attitude regarding the people called Methodists is also reflected by more scholarly writers such as Wilhelm Paulk: "They are not hostile to theology but they relegate theological responsibility to a minor place in the life of both the church and individual Christian."[2]

We may not appreciate such references, but perhaps we who are heirs of the Wesleyan heritage are, in part, to blame. "For a long time now," Schubert Ogden admits, "I have had the distinct impression that the body of Christians who boast of a *Discipline* are among the most undisciplined persons in Christendom, especially when it comes to matters of doctrine."[3]

Yet some would maintain that it is precisely from John Wesley that such disregard for matters of doctrine springs. It is true that the early biographers of Wesley pictured him as a leader of a revival who was not very interested in theology, an exponent of practical Christianity rather than doctrinal Christianity. However, later studies have captured the richness of the theological legacy of Wesley and the

Wesleyan Revival in a much clearer perspective. Therefore, if we who claim the Wesleyan tradition are casual in matters of doctrine, then, as Colin Williams points out, we have "departed from her earliest tradition, for Methodism represented in her origins a revival of theology as well as a revival of life, and the former was inseparable from the latter."[4]

"Opinions and Doctrines"

There are several factors that have played a part in this popular attitude toward Methodists and theology. The most significant influence is Wesley's admonition to "think and let think." He used this expression frequently, such as, "the distinguishing marks of a Methodist are not his opinions of any sort. . . . We think and let think."[5]

However, most persons who use this quotation fail to make the distinction that was so crucial for Wesley between opinions and essential doctrines. In his sermon on the death of George Whitefield, Wesley declared: "Let us keep close to the grand scriptural doctrines which he everywhere delivered. There are many doctrines of a less essential nature with regard to which even the sincere children of God . . . are and have been divided for many ages. In these we may think and let think; we may 'agree to disagree.' But, meantime, let us hold fast the essentials of 'the faith which was once delivered unto the saints. . . .'"[6]

Wesley's relationship with George Whitefield provides a good example of his attitude. Wesley and Whitefield disagreed strongly on the doctrine of election and predestination. Both were convinced that the other was absolutely wrong. Neither was ever able to persuade the other one to change his position. Yet they respected one another and worked together for the cause of Christ.

While Wesley always refused to draw up a creed containing a definite number of fundamental doctrines, he did list on several occasions those doctrines that were most essential in his mind. A study of his preaching also indicates those doctrines which, while he might assume their truth, he did not see as the crucial doctrines of the church. For instance, he has no sermons on the virgin birth, inspiration, or second coming.

Wesley's "think and let think" attitude and his refusal to formulate an official confession led to the absence of doctrinal requirements for membership in early Methodist societies. The sole condition for membership was the desire on the part of persons "to flee from the wrath to come, and to be saved from their sins."

About this approach Wesley commented, "The Methodists alone do not insist on your holding this or that opinion; but they think and let think. . . . Now, I do not know any religious society, either ancient or modern, wherein such liberty of conscience is now allowed, or has been allowed, since the age of the Apostles. Here is our glorying; and a glorying peculiar to us."[7]

"Essential Truth"

Yet despite the continuing popular attitude regarding Methodists and theology and the historical factors contributing to these attitudes, it must be clearly affirmed that for John Wesley and the Wesleyan Revival theology was tremendously important. It is true that Wesley allowed great freedom of belief and wanted to avoid any controversy over minor points that might hinder the greater cause of the work of Christ. But this in no way meant that he was unconcerned with doctrine. There was an abiding concern for doctrine and theological reflection at the heart of his life and his understanding of the Christian pilgrimage.

His admonition to "think and let think" was, first of all, a charge to *think*. It did not relieve Christians of the obligation for study and reflection. Freedom *in* belief was not to be understood as freedom *from* belief, indifference to belief. Wesley said that the genuine Christian is not a person of "muddy understanding" whose mind is "all in a mist."[8]

There were no doctrinal requirements for entrance into the Methodist societies, but once persons were admitted great care was taken to teach them true doctrine. Wesley's "think and let think" statement was in reference to "opinions which do not strike at the root of Christianity." His attitude toward "essential truth" was quite adamant.

Two practical problems with which Wesley had to deal reflect anything but a casual attitude toward doctrinal integrity:

"Preaching houses" were provided in which the Methodist preachers resided, and each of these houses had a deed that contained the following clause: "In case the doctrine or practice of any preacher should, in the opinion of the major part of the trustees, be not comfortable to Mr. Wesley's *Sermons*, and *Notes on the New Testament*, on representing this another preacher shall be sent within three months."

Doctrinal Guidelines

Another example comes from an occasion when a group of Methodists in Yorkshire were concerned because of the preaching of what they considered to be "false doctrines" by the preacher. They asked Mr. Wesley if they should continue to attend the services. His reply was that they first "should attend the service of the Church as often as possible. But that, secondly, if the Minister began either to preach the absolute decrees [Calvinist doctrine of election] or to rail at and ridicule Christian perfection, they should quietly and silently go out of the church; yet attend it again the next opportunity."[9]

Wesley's approach to doctrine can be understood more clearly by recalling his use of what has become known as his Quadrilateral. Scripture, tradition, experience, and reason constitute the main sources and guidelines for Christian theology. The four are interdependent and no one can be subsumed by another. Although there is a primacy that goes with scripture, all four guidelines should instruct all our theological reflection. Wesley's Quadrilateral has had enduring significance in the Wesleyan tradition. It has provided at the same time boundaries for theological reflection and flexibility for doctrinal thinking.[10]

The following chart on page 13, developed by George E. Koehler, illustrates the interdependence of the four elements of Wesley's Quadrilateral.

A Church with a Message

For fifty years, up and down and across all of England, through 40,000 sermons John Wesley kindled and nurtured what we now know as the Wesleyan Revival. And at the heart of that revival was a theological affirmation, a message. It is this message that we are going to examine in this book.

John Wesley felt that it was a particular message from God that Methodist people are called to deliver and share with others. Events have borne out the fact that this was a significant moment in God's story of salvation, a significant moment in the history of the Christian faith, when God gave to a people called Methodists a particular word that brought a revival to life, a revival that spread to the ends of the earth.

The interdependence of the four elements of Wesley's Quadrilateral

We rely on the way of salvation given in the Bible.

We use the Bible as a touchstone in examining real or supposed revelation.

We take it as the final authority in matters of faith and practice.

✔Thus we need to study and interpret it carefully.

Roots: Protestant Reformation

Danger: bibliolatry

✔We revere the ancient church as well as our own.

We use the writings of Christians through the centuries.

Particular value is given to the early church fathers.

The standards of the Church of England are utilized: prayerbook, and homilies.

Roots: Roman Catholic Church

Danger: traditionalism

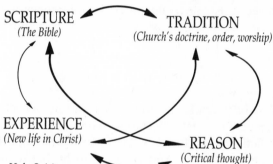

SCRIPTURE
(The Bible)

TRADITION
(Church's doctrine, order, worship)

EXPERIENCE
(New life in Christ)

REASON
(Critical thought)

✱The Holy Spirit uses scripture and tradition to bring us to faith.

✶By God's grace we receive a personal experience of faith.

There are variations of Christian experience; none can be normative.

✔Thus ours is a "heart religion," but it is not dependent on "feelings."

Roots: free churches

Danger: "enthusiasm"

✶ Reason lays the foundation for true religion and helps raise its supersturcture.

✔Reason helps us order the evidence of revelation and (with tradition) guard against poor interpretation of scripture.

✔But reason cannot prove or desclose God.

Roots: deism

Danger: rationalism

And the reason the Wesleyan Revival flourished was because of the message.

As I attend meetings of the General Board of Global Ministries of The United Methodist Church and see representatives from many nations of the world, I remember that they are there for the same reason that I am there: We have heard a message that began with Wesley's interpretation of the grace of God, and, because of the truth of that message, lives in every corner of the world have been changed.

Augustine Birrell, the nineteenth century Englishman of letters and a cabinet minister, said of John Wesley: "No other man did such a life work for England."[11] And the reason for this life achievement was the message that God put on his heart.

Questions for Thought and Discussion

1. Some say we are casual and undisciplined in our approach to doctrine. How important is careful understanding of Christian belief in your congregation? In your life?

2. John Wesley made a distinction between "opinions" (where wide differences in belief are inevitable) and "essential truths" (basic doctrines to which all Christians should adhere). But which is which? Make a list of ten opinions and ten essential doctrines. Compare your list with another person's.

3. Do you believe we in the Wesleyan tradition have a message for the world? What is it?

THE IMAGE OF GOD AND ORIGINAL SIN

The first source for Wesley's doctrine of human sinfulness is the Bible. Wesley relied particularly on the Genesis account of the garden of Eden and the "Fall" of Adam. The second source is experience. Wesley's experience confirmed what the Bible teaches in Genesis. He looked about and saw ample evidence to support the biblical belief in the utter sinfulness of persons. Tradition and reason also confirmed for Wesley this biblical understanding.

Created in God's Image

Wesley found in Genesis a state of perfection existent before the Fall, a state in which persons gave full expression to the image of God ("imago Dei") in which they were created.

In his sermon entitled "Justification by Faith," Wesley talked about this state of perfection in the following terms: "In the image of God was man made; holy as He that created him is holy; merciful as the Author of all is merciful; perfect as his Father in Heaven is perfect. As God is love, so man, dwelling in love, dwelt in God, and God in him. God made him to be an 'image of His own eternity,' an incorruptible picture of the God of glory. He was accordingly pure, as God is pure, from every spot of sin. He knew not evil in any kind or degree, but was inwardly and outwardly sinless and undefiled. He 'loved the Lord his God with all his heart, and with all his mind, and soul, and strength.'"[1]

According to Wesley, this image of God had three aspects: the natural image, political image, and moral image. The natural image involves immortality, free will, understanding, various affections, and immunity to pain. The political image means that humans are to govern over the lower beings. The moral image means that humans are created in holiness and righteousness; it involves love, justice, mercy, truth, and purity.

As Wesley put it, "So God created man in His own image, in the image of God created He him: —not barely in his *natural image*, a picture of His own immortality; a spiritual being, endued with understanding, freedom of will, and various affections; nor merely in his *political image*, the governor of this lower world, having 'dominion over the fishes of the sea, and over all the earth': but chiefly in his *moral image*; which, according to the Apostle, is 'righteousness and true holiness' (Eph. 4:24). In this image of God was man made."[2]

The moral image is the most important since it is here that humans resemble God most distinctively. The moral image also provides the chief distinction setting humans apart from other creatures.

"What then is the barrier between men and brutes? The line which they cannot pass?" asked

Wesley. His answer: "It was not reason. Set aside that ambiguous term: Exchange it for the plain word, understanding: And who can deny that brutes have this? We may as well deny that they have sight or hearing. But it is this: Man is capable of God; the inferior creatures are not. We have no ground to believe that they are, in any degree, capable of knowing, loving, or obeying God. This is the specific difference between man and brute; the great gulf which they cannot pass over."[3]

The Fall

But this state of perfection did not continue. Because of Adam's misuse of free will (the Fall), the state of perfection was almost completely lost. While the political image was not lost, part of the natural image was lost. Yet it is in regard to the moral image—the most important aspect of the image of God—that the greatest injury was suffered. So, in one sense, "everything" was lost in the Fall since the heart of the image of God had been lost. For Wesley this meant total depravity (but not, as Albert Outler puts it, "tee-total depravity," thanks to Wesley's allowance for prevenient grace and human freedom).

The will became diseased in the Fall and remained in this diseased condition. The Fall had meaning for Wesley in many ways, but, in particular, it had theological meaning. It meant that the original state of nature, as created in God's image, no longer existed.

Wesley said of Adam in regard to the Fall, "In that moment he lost the moral image of God, and, in part, the natural: He commenced unholy, foolish, and unhappy. And 'in Adam all died': He entitled all his posterity to error, guilt, sorrow, fear, pain, diseases, and death."[4]

For Wesley, sin was basic and pervaded all humankind. "Man's heart," as Wesley preached at Oxford, "is altogether corrupt and abominable." Depravity was total in this sense. Both the biblical witness and his own experience bore witness to this fact.

Wesley listed example after example from history to prove his point. Then, building on these illustrations, he said, "The preceding texts were brought to prove (and they do abundantly prove it) that our nature is deeply corrupted, inclined to evil, and disinclined to all that is spiritually good; so that, without supernatural grace, we can neither will nor do what is pleasing to God. And this easily accounts for the wickedness and misery of mankind in all ages and nations; whereby experience and reason do so strongly confirm this scriptural doctrine of original sin."[5]

There were two prongs to sin for Wesley. These two prongs were original sin and actual sins.

Original sin is the state of sin, which afflicts everyone. It is inherited and, therefore, none escapes its influence. One cannot conquer it alone;

one must accept the work of Christ. On the other hand, actual sins are *willful* transgressions of the known law of God. These are unethical acts that separate persons from God. It is even possible, according to Wesley, for actual sins to change with different times. When Wesley said, "all men are sinners," he was referring to original sin. When he said, "going on to perfection," he was referring to the victory over actual sins.

Sin and Grace

Later, as we examine Wesley's understanding of grace, we shall see how he combined in his theology this pessimism about human beings caught in original sin with an optimism about our possibilities in response to grace. Both are important.

However, we need to acknowledge today this inherent pull present in all human beings, a pull away from what ought to be. With Wesley and Paul, we need to understand what sin is. The heart of it all is this basic pull of Adam's sin—the sin of overreaching, trying to be what we cannot, being dissatisfied with being human, demanding that we be God.

Why is it that in our day the noted psychiatrist, Karl Menninger, has to ask, *Whatever Became of Sin*? There is something within us that we must understand, or ignore to our own peril. Reinhold Niebuhr says of original sin, ". . . The doctrine makes an important contribution to any adequate social and political theory the lack of which has robbed bourgeois theory of real wisdom; for it emphasizes a fact which every page of human history attests."[6]

Yet, however great our need to come to grips with Wesley's pessimism of nature, even greater is our need to recapture his optimism of grace. God's grace is sufficient. The strength of sin is overcome by the power of God's love, mercy, and forgiveness. John Wesley could affirm with great joy Paul's triumphant cry, "Where sin abounded, grace did much more abound" (Rom. 5:20).

Charles Wesley captured the freeing power of God's redemptive grace in these verses from "O For a Thousand Tongues to Sing":

> O for a thousand tongues to sing
> My great Redeemer's praise,
> The glories of my God and King,
> The triumphs of his grace!
>
> He breaks the power of canceled sin,
> He sets the prisoner free;
> His blood can make the foulest clean;
> His blood availed for me.

While many in Wesley's day found the tension between sin and grace inconsistent, Albert Outler has affirmed in recent times, "It strikes me as corresponding to some of the best we know in current psychotherapy about the human flaw and the human potential."[7] And it makes sense as I know my life. It gives some understanding to what I know about myself: that pull away from God's purpose and that pull toward the possibilities which God has for me. Perhaps it makes sense to you in what you know about yourself.

Let's pursue it further.

Questions for Thought and Discussion

1. What does "made in God's image" mean to you?

2. How do you interpret "the Fall"? What has been lost, and why? When does the Fall happen: in ancient history, once in the life of each person, every day for all of us?

3. Wesley distinguishes between original sin and actual sins. Describe this distinction. Explore the relationship between a specific sinful act on your part and your "fall" from the image of God in which you were created.

PREVENIENT GRACE AND REPENTANCE

The Christian pilgrimage is far from easy, and Wesley never oversimplified the road to salvation. His own personal agony and struggle guarded against any casual treatment of complex spiritual and human issues.

God's Initiative

Though Wesley began his understanding of humanity with original sin, he knew that sin is not what God wants for us. God is not content for us to experience nothing of life but the pull of original sin. So God comes to us, even in our sinfulness, with grace.

The beginning of the work of salvation is God's prevenient grace. The word *prevenient* simply means "to come before." It is an elemental form of grace found in everyone. It anticipates and prepares us for the coming of saving grace. This prevenient grace implies some "tendency toward life; some degree of salvation; the beginning of a deliverance from a blind, unfeeling heart."[1]

Wesley liked to talk about grace being free for all and free in all. "Free for all" means it is available to everyone (as opposed to predestination). "Free in all" refers to this prevenient grace which "waiteth not for the call." We do not have to ask for it, or even desire it. It is simply there.

Wesley understood and explained conscience (or "natural conscience," as he put it) in terms of prevenient grace. Everyone, contended Wesley, "feels more or less uneasy when he acts contrary to the light of his own conscience. So that no man sins because he has not grace, but because he does not use the grace which he hath."

While maintaining that all persons receive this prevenient grace, Wesley did allow for the practical loss of this gift by someone who has "quenched the Spirit." This occurs when, year after year, the movement of God's grace within a life is rejected. A person finally becomes deadened to the promptings of God, though no life ever moves outside the realm of God's own love and care.

God comes to us first. That is the significance of prevenient grace. God seeks us before we ever seek God. The initiative of salvation is with God from the very beginning. Before we ever take a step, God is there. Within every life, from the very beginning, is this simple, basic, elemental presence and movement of God.

This prevenient grace gives the power to respond to God. It gives the power to respond positively by accepting the fuller expressions of God's grace, or negatively by rejecting God's call. In this formulation, Wesley combined in a significant way the two thrusts of divine initiative and human response.

In the midst of controversy between a Calvinistic theology emphasizing divine initiative and a Catholic theology stressing human response, Wesley brought these two dimensions of the God-human encounter together through prevenient grace. God acts first in prevenient grace, which gives us the power to respond without dictating our response.

And respond we must. Prevenient grace is not enough. Prevenient grace gives us a sense of God but is in no sense the totality of God's grace. Prevenient grace only serves to stir us to repentance, which Wesley calls the porch of religion.

The entrance to the life of faith is repentance, and it is prevenient grace that leads to repentance. "Stir up the spark of grace which is now in you," he said, "and he will give you more grace."[2] Later we will see how justifying grace and sanctifying grace are possible only because we have been empowered by God's initiative of prevenient grace.

Repentance

The Christian life cannot begin without a person's acknowledgment of sin. Repentance, or conviction of sin, always precedes faith. Prevenient grace makes this recognition of the fallen state possible. Repentance is not so much remorse as it is true self-understanding. "Repent," said Wesley, "that is, know yourselves . . . know thyself to be a sinner, and what manner of sinner thou art."[3]

The famous letter of the Duchess of Buckingham to Lady Huntingdon gives a clue about the importance of this theme in the preaching of the Wesleyan Revival. The doctrines of the Methodist preachers, she wrote, "are most repulsive and strongly tinctured with impertinence and disrespect toward their superiors in perpetually endeavoring to level all ranks and do away with all distinctions, as it is monstrous to be told that you have a heart as sinful as the common wretches that crawl on the earth."[4]

In addition to self-knowledge, repentance involves an earnest desire to escape from one's present condition and enter the door of the kingdom of God. Then it is that faith comes as the gift of God, a gift most graciously received because first it has been most fervently desired.

Does this imply a justification by faith *and* works, or an actual cooperation between God and persons in salvation? Not unless one forgets the basic context in which human responsiveness is set, the prevenient grace of God. Thus, our human response is not because of any inherent ability but because of the prior presence of God's grace in our lives. However, human response is essential. Persons must actively respond to God's gracious offer of the free gift of faith, the sole condition of justification, by reaching out with the arms of repentance to receive that gift.[5]

It is with this background that we are able to consider the basic Wesleyan theme of justification by faith.

Questions for Thought and Discussion

1. God's "prevenient grace," according to Wesley, "comes before" any act on our part, helps us recognize our fallen state, and gives us the power to respond to God. Describe examples of this aspect of God's love in your life.

2. For Wesley, repentance is self-knowledge and a desire to escape from one's present condition. Consider the story of the prodigal son as an example of repentance (especially Luke 15:17-19). What has been your own experience of repentance?

JUSTIFICATION BY FAITH

John Wesley regarded salvation through faith as "the fundamental doctrine of the church." In 1738, eighteen days after his conversion experience, Wesley delivered the sermon, "Salvation by Faith," at St. Mary's Church in Oxford. It is a fact—the central fact in the Wesleyan Revival—that from 1738 onwards, Wesley taught *sola fide* (by faith alone, Romans 1:17) as the first and last article by which the church (and with it the gospel) stands or falls. Having once understood this principle of salvation by faith, Wesley never deviated from it.[1]

Faith in Jesus Christ

Wesley began his famous sermon on salvation by faith by spelling out what faith is not. It is not the faith of a heathen who merely believes that some kind of God exists. Nor is it the faith of a devil who believes and fears a just punishment. Neither is it a speculative, rational thing, a cold, lifeless assent, a train of ideas in the head. Faith is a disposition of the heart.

The proper object of faith is Jesus Christ, who has acted mightily for our salvation. Salvation is made possible by the grace of God given freely to all who have faith in Christ.

G. C. Cell is right when he calls the Atonement the "burning focus of faith" for Wesley. For just as Wesley placed great stress on the doctrine of original sin in order to make it clear that it is only by God's grace that persons can be saved, so he also placed his central emphasis on the Atonement to make it clear that it is only at great cost that God has provided the grace by which we can be forgiven.[2]

As Albert Outler puts it: "In a hundred different ways on thousands of different occasions, decade after five decades, his one consistent message was Jesus Christ and him crucified—*Christus crucifixus, Christus redemptor, Christus victor.*"[3] Salvation is possible, clearly, because of the grace of God and, therefore, not something for which we can claim credit. "Of yourselves cometh neither your faith nor your salvation: 'It is the gift of God'; the free, undeserved gift."[4]

Free Grace

Wesley was in agreement with John Calvin on most issues but not on the subject of predestination. One of the recurring notes of the Wesleyan Revival was sounded by Wesley in his sermon on free grace, namely, that the good news of the gospel is that God's grace or love is "free in all and free for all." Wesley made constant and vigorous attacks against predestination, a doctrine which he "abhored."

Of the various arguments which Wesley developed against predestination, five of the most important may be summarized.

1. The doctrine makes vain the preaching of the gospel—which God has commanded—since the aim of preaching is to save souls, but the elect will be saved without preaching, and the nonelect cannot be saved with it.

2. Predestination tends to overthrow and make unnecessary the whole Christian revelation, since persons who are saved or damned according to eternal, unchangeable decrees cannot be affected by the gospel. But a gospel that is not necessary is not true, and, thus, the whole Christian cause is sacrificed.

3. The doctrine destroys zeal for good works, since it tends to lessen our love for the majority of persons—"the evil and the unthankful"—and our concern for their spiritual and material needs.

4. It is based on an interpretation of a limited number of biblical texts which contradict other passages and "the whole scope and tenor of Scripture."

5. It blasphemes and dishonors God, undermining God's truth, justice, and love. The God implied in this doctrine is more false, unjust, and cruel than the devil, condemning multitudes and dooming to perdition many persons who earnestly desire salvation.[5]

Wesley's attacks on predestination, while interesting from a historical perspective, are not nearly so helpful today as many of his other theological perspectives. Few today hold to predestination in the form against which Wesley argued. Furthermore, ecumenical discussions are not helped by such characterizations of Calvinistic theology which do not adequately capture the important positive intent of this doctrine, namely its witness to the sovereignty of God.

Free grace, for Wesley, has the following characteristics:

1. Grace is a gift grounded in God's free act in Christ.

2. Grace is free for all; the atonement contains a universal invitation.

3. Grace is free in all; prevenient goodness leads and strengthens every person.

4. Grace is free in salvation, independent of any merit or work.

5. Grace is free to accomplish full salvation, consummated in entire sanctification and Christian perfection.[6]

While always holding that the very power by which persons turn to God comes from God as a gift, Wesley also maintained free choice: that all are free to choose and, in order to be saved, *must* choose.

Falling from Grace and Cheap Grace

Wesley held that freedom of choice is still possible after one's initial decision to accept the gift of salvation. In other words, "falling from grace" is a possibility in the Christian life. Perhaps "departing from grace" might be a more appropriate way to speak of this theological reality. Bishop Mack B. Stokes refers to falling from grace as a doctrine which Methodists preach and everyone practices.

Wesley fully recognized the danger of what Bonhoeffer has called "cheap grace."[7] For this reason he stressed that faith requires the opening of the believer's life to the work of God. Justification is not a state but a moment-by-moment relationship of faith and response.

Justification is the beginning of the Christian life, and no matter how glorious, dramatic, or life-changing it is, it still remains a beginning. Justification represents the door of true religion. Wesley fully expected believers to walk through the door.

Faith, far from being a static concept for Wesley, was a dynamic reality. Faith cannot be understood apart from faithfulness. Good works cannot save, but they are the inevitable fruit of saving faith. "To turn the grace of God into an encouragement to sin, is the sure way to the nethermost hell!"[8]

Results

One result of justification is a joy in our faith. Wesley came to see that. Prior to 1738 he had the "faith of a servant," after that time he had the "faith of a son."

Another result is a freedom to live as free persons—not perfect, but accepted and forgiven by a gracious God. By acknowledging our condition as sinners, there is no longer any need to defend ourselves because we are not perfect. There is no longer any need to compare our righteousness with that of others.

Here is found a genuine freedom to act. No longer are we prevented from acting for fear that our actions may be inadequate or even wrong. Facing honestly our own incompleteness and deficiencies, we can reach out to confront problems according to the best light we have, sustained by the knowledge that we are saved by God's grace and not our own judgment or righteousness.[9]

Other results of justification such as love, works, generosity, personal and social holiness, will be explored in later chapters. First we will consider how we come to know that we are saved.

Questions for Thought and Discussion

1. Compare "faith in Jesus Christ" with various current misunderstandings of "faith."

2. Today belief in "predestination" no longer keeps many people from accepting the free gift of God's grace. But what *are* some of these blocks to faith in our time?

3. For Wesley, the faith that leads to salvation is both a gift of God and a choice on our part. Describe the two sides of this divine-human act as you have experienced it.

4. What have been some of the results of faith for you? What fruits have you expected and longed for but not yet received?

THE WITNESS OF THE SPIRIT

Paul's claim that the "Spirit itself bears witness with our Spirit, that we are children of God" (Rom. 8:16) is the centerpiece of Wesley's understanding of the witness of the Spirit, commonly known as the doctrine of assurance.

Bishop William R. Cannon describes Wesley's doctrine of assurance as "Methodism's most distinctive doctrinal characteristic." Wesley regarded the witness of the Spirit as "one grand part of the testimony which God has given" the Methodists to bear to all humankind.[1]

Assurance

What is this doctrine?

According to Wesley's definition, "The testimony of the Spirit is an inward impression on the souls of believers, whereby the Spirit of God directly testifies to their Spirit, that they are children of God."[2] It is "inward consciousness" of sins forgiven, joy of life, acceptance by God, and assurance of salvation.

Does justification necessarily imply assurance?

Although Wesley once held that justification and assurance always go together, experience led him to discard the view that there could be no salvation without assurance. He still held that persons normally receive the witness of the Spirit as soon as they believe. Thus, in his answer to Professor Rutherford in 1768, he said, "I believe a consciousness of being in the favour of God (which I do not term *full assurance*, since it is frequently weakened, nay, perhaps interrupted, by returns of doubts or fear) is the common privilege of Christians, fearing God and working righteousness. Yet I do not affirm there are no exceptions to this general rule . . . therefore I have not, for many years, thought a consciousness of acceptance to be essential to justifying faith."[3]

Wesley's Own Experience

In addition to his evidence from the Bible, Wesley came to this emphasis from his mind and his experience.

It was from the Moravians, and especially from the teaching of Peter Böhler that Wesley in the early part of 1738 learned that one of the fruits of true faith in Christ is "constant peace, arising from a sense of forgiveness." "I was quite amazed," he said in his *Journal*, "and looked upon it as a new gospel" (although the concept was not completely new to him).[4]

His own experience led him to embrace this doctrine of assurance. A crisis resulted in his life as he accepted with his mind a doctrine that pointed to an experience he did not yet have as a living reality in his life.

Then came his May 24, 1738, experience of attending, in an initially depressed state of mind, the meeting of a religious society at Nettleton Court, off Aldersgate Street in London. There, after listening to the reading of a translation of Luther's preface to Paul's *Epistle to the Romans*, he rose to testify to what he felt to be a great moment in his spiritual pilgrimage. His *Journal* entry reads: "I felt my heart strangely warmed. I felt I did trust in Christ, Christ alone for salvation; and an assurance was given me that He had taken away *my* sins, even *mine*, and saved *me* from the law of sin and death."

The "Aldersgate experience" has been greatly exaggerated through the years as a decisive boundary between Wesley's life before and after that point (despite his post-Aldersgate *Journal* entries that defy such simplification). Yet it is true that something occurred in that experience which had a profound effect on Wesley and those who have followed in the Wesleyan tradition.

In this doctrine, perhaps more so than any other, one confronts the profound and crucial role of religious experience in Christian faith, a theme at the heart of the Wesleyan Revival. Repeated references to experience in Wesley's preaching reflect his firm conviction that God can be directly and personally known. Experience also provides powerful evidence for the truth of the Christian message. In his Sixth

University Sermon, he spoke of "the sure test of experience."

But the test must never be confused with the source. Wesley successfully avoids the pitfalls of subjectivism by combining personal experience with his other tests for religious truth, scripture and reason. While experience is suspect if it stands alone, experience remained indispensable for Wesley, who felt that no religious teaching means very much unless its claims are experientially validated. The truth that saves and transforms is the truth that is personally appropriated. "The image of God impressed on a created spirit"—this is "the strongest evidence of the truth of Christianity."[5]

Roots and Fruits

Wesley was careful to insist that assurance is more than a feeling. If Wesley countered "mere formality" (the form of godliness without the power of it) with his emphasis on religious experience, he also opposed "the wildness of enthusiasm" by keeping in perspective the role of emotion. Fearing that dependence on emotion might lead persons to mistake pious imaginings for the witness of the Spirit of God, Wesley made two points to separate assurance from mere emotion or feelings:

First, the testimony of God's Spirit precedes the testimony of our own spirit. The testimony of the Spirit is an inward impression of the soul. The

Christian is aware of being grasped by God's Spirit. This awareness may bring feelings, but its authenticity is not explainable in terms of sense experience.

There is a spiritual power in assurance which is able to sustain one even when feelings are low. The Christian "may start, tremble, change colour, or be otherwise disordered in body while the soul is calmly stayed on God and remains in perfect peace. Nay, the mind itself may be deeply distressed, may be exceeding sorrowful, may be perplexed and pressed down by heaviness and anguish, even to agony, while the heart cleaves to God by perfect love and the will is wholly resigned to Him. Was it not so with the Son of God Himself?"[6]

Second, there are fruits of the Spirit. Wesley warned against "any supposed testimony of the Spirit which is separate from the fruit of it."[7] If one's experience is with the living God, rather than a passing emotion, then changes will be produced. I am reminded of Dwight L. Moody's comment, "It's not how loud you shout or how high you jump, it's how straight you walk when you come down that counts."

The danger that this emphasis will lead to a salvation by works is minimal so long as one remembers that the assurance is not that we are perfect or even worthy, but that we are forgiven and accepted by God.

The heart of this doctrine is that each of us can experience an assurance of our acceptance by God. For some of us this confidence comes gradually. For others it comes as a sudden discovery at the moment of faith. For all of us it brings a peace and calm for our lives. What a blessed gift of God!

Next let's look at the place of the church in the Christian pilgrimage.

Questions for Thought and Discussion

1. Some people seem more assured of God's grace and their own faith than others, a difference which Wesley eventually came to acknowledge. You may know people who seem to have more faith than assurance (and perhaps some with more assurance than faith!). What has been your own history of assurance, its ups and downs? Describe one experience in which you were certain of God's love and your own faithful response.

2. Assurance is not equivalent to positive feelings. Can you recall a time when you were "down," yet still certain of God's saving love? How about a time when you were both "up" and assured?

3. What is the role of doubt in genuine faith?

The Church and the Christian Life

John Wesley had an exceedingly strong doctrine of the church. He also had a deep passion for unity in the church and loyalty to the Church of England. Not only did he refuse to allow the Methodist societies to separate from the Church of England, but he always insisted that society meetings not conflict with established church services. On occasions when societies were informed of conflicting services, the societies concluded their meetings so persons could attend the Church of England worship and celebrate Holy Communion.

In revising the Articles of Religion of the Church of England for Methodists in America, Wesley left unchanged the article on the church: "The visible Church of Christ is a congregation of faithful men in which the pure Word of God is preached, and the Sacraments duly administered according to Christ's ordinance, in all those things that of necessity are requisite to the same."[1]

Wesley singles out three things that are essential to a visible church: "First: Living faith; without which, indeed, there can be no church at all, neither visible or invisible. Secondly: Preaching, and consequently hearing, the pure word of God, else that faith would languish and die. And, Thirdly, a due administration of the Sacraments,—the ordinary means whereby God increaseth faith."[2]

"Means of Grace"

It is in the context of the church that Christian growth takes place through the various means of grace. Wesley was convinced that vital spiritual life was only possible as a person opened his or her life to the means of grace in a community of faith. Wesley defined means of grace as "outward signs, words, actions, ordained of God, and appointed for this end, to be the ordinary channels whereby he might convey to men, preventing, justifying, or sanctifying grace."[3]

Reminiscent of the plea in Ephesians to "put on all the armour which God provides" (Eph. 6:10, NEB), Wesley calls on persons at every opportunity to "use all the means which God has ordained." While acknowledging dependence upon God's grace, Wesley says the real question is whether we are going to wait for the grace of God by "using these means or by laying them aside." However, Wesley had to admit that a constant temptation is present to mistake means for ends, to seek justification through works. For this reason he issued guidelines for the right use of the means of grace.[4]

First, always retain a lively sense that God is above all means. Do not limit the Almighty. God does whatsoever and whensoever it pleases God to do.

God can convey grace either in or out of any of the means. Always look at every moment for God's appearing. God is always ready, able, and willing to save.

Second, before using any means, let it be deeply impressed on your soul that there is no power in this. It is, in itself, a poor, dead, empty thing. Separate from God, it is a shadow. There is nothing in it intrinsically pleasing to God whereby favor is gained. The work itself profits nothing if you trust not in God alone.

Third, in using all means, seek God alone. In and through every outward means, look singly to the power of God's Spirit and the merits of God's Son. Do not stay with the work itself; nothing short of God can satisfy your soul. Remember always to use all means *as means*, as ordained, not for their own sake, but for the renewal of your soul in righteousness and true holiness.

Last, after you have used any of these means, take care how you value yourself and so not congratulate yourself as having done some great thing. Such will turn all to poison.

Piety

What, then, are the means of grace? Wesley divided them into two categories: instituted means of grace (or works of piety) and prudential means of grace (or words of mercy). The instituted means of grace included prayer, scripture, the Lord's Supper, fasting, and Christian conference. Here are summaries of these, using Wesley's words.

Prayer. God commands all who desire to receive any grace to pray. All who desire the grace of God are to wait for it in the way of prayer. This is the express direction of our Lord. In the Sermon on the Mount Jesus puts it in the simplest terms: "Ask, and it shall be given you; seek, and ye shall find; knock, and it shall be opened unto you: for every one that asketh receiveth; and he that seeketh findeth; and to him that knocketh it shall be opened."[5]

Scripture. Searching the scriptures includes hearing, reading, and meditating upon God's Word. This is the means whereby God not only gives but also confirms and increases true wisdom. We can learn from Paul's words to Timothy: "From a child thou hast known the Holy Scriptures, which are able to make thee wise unto salvation through faith which is in Christ Jesus" (2 Tim. 3:15). Neither the learned nor the unlearned are saved from the trouble of thinking. All are to think. This is the way to understand the things of God. Meditate day and night.

Some of Wesley's suggestions for the most effective reading of scripture: (1) set apart a little time every morning and evening for that purpose; (2) at each time read a chapter out of the Old Testament and one out of the New Testament; (3) read with a fixed resolution to know and do the whole will of God; (4) have a constant eye for connection with the grand doctrines of the faith; (5) pray before and following reading; and (6) pause throughout reading to examine your heart and life.

What if a passage is difficult to understand? The general rule of interpreting scripture is this: the literal sense of every text is to be taken, if it is not contrary to some other texts; but in that case the obscure text is to be interpreted by those which speak more plainly and clearly to the subject matter of the obscure passage.[6]

The Lord's Supper. All who desire an increase of the grace of God are to wait for it in partaking of the Lord's Supper. This is the direction of our Lord: "Do this in remembrance of me." Paul put it this way: "For as often as ye eat this bread, and drink this cup, ye do show forth the Lord's death till He come."

While many affirm that the Lord's Supper is not converting, only confirming, experience shows the falsehood of such thinking. Many persons know that their first conviction of sin was wrought at the Lord's Supper. The Lord's Supper was ordained by God to be a means of conveying to persons either preventing, justifying, or sanctifying grace, according to their particular needs. The persons for whom it was ordained are all who know and feel that they need the grace of God. No fitness is required but a sense of our state of utter sinfulness and helplessness.[7]

Fasting. Of all the means of grace there is scarcely any concerning which persons have run into greater extremes than that of religious fasting. Some have exalted this beyond all scripture and reason while others have utterly disregarded it. The truth lies between them both. It is not the end but it is a precious means which God has ordained and which, properly used, will bring God's blessing. It is certain that our Master did not imagine fasting to be a little thing.

Every time of fasting, either public or private, should be a season of exercising all of those holy affections which are implied in a broken and contrite heart. Let it be a season of devout mourning, of godly sorrow for sin. And with fasting should be joined fervent prayer, pouring out our whole souls before God, confessing our sins, humbling ourselves, laying open before him all our wants, guilt, and helplessness. It is a time for enlarging our prayers on behalf of others.[8]

Christian conference. Wesley's emphasis on fellowship and nurture through small groups deserves special consideration in the next chapter, along with the "prudential means of grace" (or works of mercy).

Questions for Thought and Discussion

1. Although we know better, we sometimes do "good works" as if we could thereby earn God's grace. What are three or four examples in your life? How do Wesley's guidelines for using the "means of grace" (p. 25) apply to these?

2. How do you evaluate Wesley's suggestions for daily Bible study (p. 26)? What would your own list of suggestions look like?

3. Consider the role in your life of the four "works of piety" outlined in this chapter: prayer, scripture, the Lord's Supper, and fasting. Is each serving as a means of God's grace in your own growth? What changes might you make?

GROWTH THROUGH CHRISTIAN COMMUNITY

While conversion was always the chief aim of preaching in the Wesleyan Revival, Wesley was equally emphatic about the place of Christian nurture. "Converts without nurture are like stillborn babies." "Follow the blow," he said. "Never encourage the devil by snatching souls from him that you cannot nurture."[1] About the vulnerability of unnurtured converts he wrote in his *Journal*, "I was more convinced than ever that the preaching like an Apostle, without joining together those that are awakened and training them up to the ways of God, is only begetting children for the murderer."[2]

Wesley believed that the necessity for mutual encouragement, examination, and service, within the context of the means of grace, required more than hearing the Word and participating in the sacraments. He felt the Church of England did not sufficiently provide for the fellowship of Christian people, which he sensed to have been a unique characteristic of the early church.

Speaking of the failure of true fellowship in the Church of England, Wesley wrote, "Look east or west, north or south; name what parish you please: is this Christian fellowship there? Rather, are not the bulk of parishioners a mere rope of sand? What Christian connection is there between them? What intercourse in spiritual things? What watching over each other's souls? What bearing of one another's burdens?"[3]

Class Meetings

So Wesley set out to "introduce fellowship where it was utterly destroyed." He believed that his class meeting represented the genius of primitive Christianity and that God had given him a vision of the way in which these groups could be the means of spreading scriptural holiness throughout the land.[4]

The class meetings were neither rivals to nor substitutes for the church and its ministry. Rather, the small groups complemented the church by offering a more intense and personal encounter of faith and grace within a context of mutual support, love, and care. Not only did this system of nurture conserve the results of the revival preaching, but it also became the principal avenue of pastoral care during the Wesleyan Revival.[5]

Relying on James 5:16 ("Confess your faults one to another, and pray one for another, that ye may be healed"), Wesley issued goals for the groups. Below are Wesley's directives, in his words:

"1. To meet once a week, at the least.

2. To come punctually at the hour appointed, without some extraordinary reason.

3. To begin (those of us who are present) exactly at the hour, with singing or prayer.

4. To speak each of us in order, freely and plainly, the true state of our souls, with the faults we have committed in thought, word, or deed, and the temptations we have felt since our last meeting.

5. To end every meeting with prayer suited to the state of each person present.

6. To desire some person among us to speak his own state first, and then to ask the rest, in order, as many and as searching questions as may be, concerning their state, sins and temptations.

Some of the questions proposed to every one before he is admitted among us may be to this effect:

1. Have you the forgiveness of your sins?

2. Have you peace with God through our Lord Jesus Christ?

3. Have you the witness of God's Spirit with your spirit that you are a child of God?

4. Is the love of God shed abroad in your heart?

5. Has no sin, inward or outward, dominion over you?

6. Do you desire to be told of your faults?

7. Do you desire to be told of all your faults . . .?

8. Do you desire that every one of us should tell you, from time to time, whatsoever is in his heart concerning you?

9. Consider! Do you desire we should tell you whatsoever we think, whatsoever we fear, whatsoever we hear concerning you?

10. Do you desire that, in doing this, we should come as close as possible; that we should cut to the quick, and search your heart to the bottom?

11. Is it your desire and design to be, on this and all other occasions, entirely open, so as to speak everything that is in your heart without exception, without disguise and without reserve?

Any of the preceding questions may be asked as often as occasion offers; the five following at every meeting:

1. What known sins have you committed since our last meeting?
2. What temptations have you met with?
3. How were you delivered?
4. What have you thought, said, or done, of which you doubt whether it be sin or not?
5. Have you nothing you desire to keep secret?"[6]

It was Wesley's feeling that every member should feel responsible for every other member. When a friend suggested that every group should have a strong leader, Wesley replied, "No, that would give him too much to do and the rest of us too little." Yet natural leadership did emerge from these groups. These leaders became quite central to the Methodist movement.

Much of the success and effectiveness of the small groups resulted from the high sense of responsibility each member assumed for every other member and for the group as a whole. Outler points out that it was in the bands (smaller groups of four or five persons) and classes (about twelve persons) that people who were faceless and worthless in the streets outside the chapel found respect, dignity, and a new vision of God and of the human possibility.

Wesley had a practice worth rediscovering. It may well be that the recovery of small groups for sharing, caring, and growing is a key ingredient in the church's becoming a real community of God's people in today's world. It is interesting to observe that the contemporary United Methodist Church in Angola, one of the fastest growing churches in the world, is using the class meeting model as its primary structure for evangelism, nurture, and Christian education.

Works of Mercy

Wesley provided further structure for the Christian pilgrimage of discipleship through the societies by proposing prudential (or variable) means of grace, realizing that the details of these, as opposed to the instituted means, would change with different circumstances. These prudential means are sometimes referred to as "works of mercy." Wesley listed these under three headings: doing no harm, doing good, and attending upon all the ordinances of God.

"Doing no harm" meant avoiding evil of every kind, especially that which is most generally practiced. For Wesley this included taking the name of God in vain, profaning the day of the Lord, using or selling liquor, fighting, quarreling, practicing usury, spending time in unprofitable conversations, and wearing gold or costly apparel.

"Doing good" meant seizing every opportunity to do good in every possible way. Giving food to the hungry and clothing to the naked, visiting the sick and imprisoned, and instructing all whom one encounters were some of Wesley's suggestions, with special emphasis being given to helping those of the household of faith. This will be explored in the chapter on social holiness.

"Attending upon all the ordinances of God" meant the public worship of God, the ministry of the word, the Lord's Supper, family and private prayer, Bible study, and fasting.[7]

It was Dietrich Bonhoeffer who said, "It is becoming clearer every day that the most urgent problem besetting our Church is this: How can we live the Christian life in the modern world?" Long before Bonhoeffer, John Wesley recognized the high cost of discipleship and sought to fashion a structure within the Christian community providing spiritual growth for persons trying to live the Christian life in the midst of what was for them a new and challenging modern world.

What, then, is the goal of Christian growth? The goal is none other than holiness of heart and life which we shall now explore.

Questions for Thought and Discussion

1. To what degree do members of your congregation "watch over each other's souls," "bear one another's burdens"? Conversely, in what sense is your church a mere "rope of sand"?

2. The questions to be used in class meetings indicate an astonishing openness with one another. Do you feel there is a need for such frank sharing in today's church? In what settings? In general, how could we incorporate the values of the class meeting in our church fellowship?

3. You might examine your life for one week, making daily entries under Wesley's three types of "works of mercy": doing no harm, doing good, attending upon all the ordinances of God. What changes would you make in order to further your Christian pilgrimage?

HOLINESS OF HEART AND LIFE

A perhaps apocryphal story is told of how on one occasion Bishop J. Lloyd Decell called in a pastor who had been disappointed in his appointment. The Bishop said, "My brother, I want you to know that this appointment has been sanctified by long hours of thought and prayer." The man replied, "Bishop, that's the strangest Methodist theology I ever heard of." The Bishop asked, "What do you mean?" and the man answered, "According to Methodist theology a thing has to be justified before it can be sanctified."[1]

The disgruntled pastor at least knew that sanctification came only after justification. The two are tied closely together in Wesleyan thought, as justifying grace led to sanctifying grace. If repentance is the door of true faith, the expectation, in Wesley's understanding of faith, is that one will not only walk through the door but also continue walking for the rest of one's life. The implications of faith and salvation continue to be worked out, producing both "inward and outward holiness," this being an essential part of the "fundamental doctrine of the people called Methodists."

The value Wesley attached to the doctrine of sanctification (also referred to as the doctrine of Christian perfection) grew even as clergy attacked it. Failure to preach it in Cornwall, he thought, had caused believers to "grow dead or cold"; in Bristol membership had fallen away because perfection had "been little insisted on"; at Tiverton it had been preached "only in general terms." Wherever it was not earnestly taught (as Wesley interpreted events), the work of God did not prosper.[2]

Sources

Wesley based his preaching on holiness, sanctification, and Christian perfection in scripture, tradition, reason, and experience.

Basing his "Christian Perfection" sermon on Philippians 3:12 ("Not that I have already obtained this or am already perfect"), he declared, "There is scarce any expression in holy writ, which has given more offence than this. . . . Whatsoever God hath spoken, that will we speak. . . . We may not, therefore, lay these expressions aside, seeing they are the words of God and not of man."[3]

Far from being contrary to the doctrine of the Church of England, Wesley understood his doctrine of perfection to be exactly the same. He reminded doubters that English clergy prayed every Sunday: "Cleanse the thoughts of our hearts by the inspiration of the Holy Spirit that we may perfectly love thee, and worthily magnify thy holy name." This reflected what he understood by perfection.

Perhaps Wesley was also remembering his own service of ordination on September 22, 1728, when

Bishop John Potter read the historic charge to elders: "Wherefore see that you never cease your labor, your care and your diligence until you have done all that lieth in you, according to your bounden duty, to bring all such as shall be committed to your charge unto perfectness in Christ."

Wesley knew, through reason, that growth is an essential part of life, built into the very fabric of existence. People are born to grow and develop.

His own experience in the spiritual journey confirmed for him the capacity and necessity of faith to grow and develop. Thus, it became essential for "growth in grace" toward the goal of Christian perfection to be at the heart of Wesleyan Revival preaching.

A reminder today of the Wesleyan stress on perfection is found in two of the historic questions asked of United Methodist clergy seeking admission to an Annual Conference: "Are you going on to perfection?" and "Do you expect to be made perfect in love in this life?"

Our oldest child, just before beginning the first grade, was reflecting on the new experience of school. "After the first grade, I'll be in the second, then the third, then. . . ." All of a sudden a look of mild panic, then resignation, covered his face. "I've sure got a long way to go!" Wesley echoed something of that sentiment in his spiritual journey. Aldersgate was not for him so much the end of a quest as it was another beginning in his search for true holiness of heart and life.

What Perfection Is Not

Wesley took care to stress what perfection is not. It is not freedom from ignorance, mistakes, temptation, physical or mental infirmities. It implies no perfection of knowledge, judgment, or action. In fact, perfection is by no means absolute. The perfect are never so perfect as to be free from the need of forgiveness.

"Absolute and infallible perfection?" Wesley asked. "I never contended for it. Sinless perfection? Neither do I contend for this, seeing the term is not scriptural. A perfection that perfectly fulfills the whole law, and so needs not the merit of Christ? I acknowledge none such—I do now, and always did, protest against it."[4]

In 1900 at a national gathering of a major Protestant denomination a delegate offered the following catalog of sinful activities: cigarette smoking, Coca-Cola guzzling, card-playing, novel reading, dancing, opera, grand opera, living pictures, tableaux, charades, prize fights, bull fights, dog fights, cock fights, yachting, roller skating, football, baseball, curling, backgammon, billiards, checkers, chess, dice, polo, croquet, pool, golf, lawn tennis, cricket, one o'cat, and shinney. This list highlights the absurdity of any supposed perfection of deeds. How does one begin to discern what the deeds are?

However, Wesley grasped the more substantive reason for avoiding such an approach to perfection. It is not in harmony with the Christian gospel of sin and grace. It is unfortunate that all too often a kind of rulebook legalism has been communicated in our churches rather than the gospel as proclaimed in the Wesleyan Revival. A recent study of the unchurched in America reveals that churches have communicated either intentionally or unwittingly to the unchurched an interpretation of the Christian gospel that has reduced it to legalistic moralisms, narrow prohibitions, and petty prescriptions of acceptable Christian behavior.[5]

So Wesley's dilemma was to define an imperfect perfection. A key is found in the meanings of two words. Although many who heard Wesley understood "perfection" in terms of the Latin word *perfectus* (a finished and complete state of attainment), Wesley understood it otherwise. He was thinking more of the meaning conveyed by the Greek verb *teleiō* (to make perfect, to fulfill), a word implying process, growth, and journey. As Charles Wesley wrote,

> "Yet when the work is done
> The work is but begun."

Perfect Love

What then was Christian perfection for Wesley? It was a perfection in love. "This is the sum of Christian perfection—loving God and loving our neighbor—these contain the whole of Christian perfection!"[6]

Wesley spoke of "inward holiness" (love of God and the assurance of God's love for us) and "outward holiness" (love of neighbor and deeds of kindness). Without ever implying sinless perfection, Wesley believed in a hope and expectation that our motives will be purified in love and thus move closer to the goal of perfect love God has for us.

Wesley was fond of speaking of persons being "happy and holy." For him the two experiences, far from being opposites, are actually one reality. "Why are not you happy?" Wesley frequently asked—only to answer, "Other circumstances may concur, but the main reason is because you are not holy."[7]

Holiness always remains a gift of grace, not a merited achievement.

The arrogance and self-righteousness that characterized the "sanctification" and "second blessing" movements in America earlier in this century caused many persons in the Wesleyan heritage to, as Outler put it, throw the Wesleyan baby of true holiness out with the "second blessing" bathwater. This is unfortunate. Sanctification, if properly understood, is a rich doctrine full of deep spiritual potential for Christians and the church. Wesley took perfection to be "the grand depositum which God has lodged with the people called Methodists; and for the sake of propagating this chiefly He appeared to have raised us up."[8]

Robert E. Chiles claims that Wesley's stress on sanctification and perfection "gives to Methodism a singular place and voice among the major Protestant traditions,"[9] and Outler believes this particular sort of linkage between *sola fide* (justification by faith alone) and "holy living" (sanctification) "has no precedent anywhere in classical Protestantism."[10] It is easy for us to miss the significance of this Wesleyan view of "faith alone" and "holy living" held together. Here was a great evangelist preaching salvation by faith and, at the same time, teaching his converts to go on to perfection.

While sanctification has often been thought of primarily in personal terms, many have seen its broader social ramifications. In 1912 C. W. Barnes wrote of a "new sanctification" involving "the redemption of society, the cleansing of the social order from all sin—that is to say, selfishness, injustice, and wrong." He went on to say that it is this "new holiness" for which the modern world prays.[11]

Today, Theodore H. Runyon and others are developing the social implications of Wesleyan holiness.[12] A peculiar affinity is seen by them between Wesleyan theology, particularly Wesley's doctrine of sanctification, and movements for social change. The goal of perfection not only engenders a fundamental hope for a better future but also arouses a holy dissatisfaction with any present state of affairs. This holy dissatisfaction is readily transferable from the realm of the individual to that of society, where it provides a persistent motivation for change.

Let's look next at how social holiness was expressed in the Wesleyan Revival.

Questions for Thought and Discussion

1. You might ask yourself the question, "Do you expect to be made perfect in love in this life?" If not, why not? If so, how are you progressing?

2. What, for you, is the relationship between "inward holiness" (love of God) and "outward holiness" (love of neighbor and deeds of kindness)? How does growth in one area affect growth in the other?

3. In your experience, how is happiness related to holiness?

4. In Wesley's view, our salvation by faith alone *must* lead us into continuing growth in holy living. In what ways is this happening and not happening in your life?

SOCIAL HOLINESS

"In our era," said Dag Hammarskjöld, "the road to holiness necessarily passes through the world of action."[1] So it was for the early Methodists.

The Wesleyan Revival was first and foremost a religious revival which stressed personal religious experience. However, from the beginning of this movement, the implications of repentance for social reform were given serious attention. "Reform of the nation" was an early stated purpose of Methodism, along with "spreading scriptural holiness over the land." In America, the linkage between faith and social responsibility can be seen in the Christmas Conference of 1784, where one of the actions was to adopt a call for the abolition of slavery.

John Wesley was clear on the unity of faith and action. "Christianity is essentially a social religion," declared Wesley, "and to turn it into a solitary religion is indeed to destroy it."[2] Or as he put it on another occasion, "The Gospel of Christ knows no religion but social; no holiness but social holiness."[3]

While the social impact of the Wesleyan Revival has often been exaggerated by succeeding generations, one can safely say that revolutionary changes in English life resulted from this movement of God. Marquis W. Childs and Douglas Cater conclude that "out of the light kindled by Wesley and the evangelical revival came the great drive for reform movements that has had a direct and continuing relationship to the life of the past 100 years." With this judgment Kenneth E. Boulding concurs, asserting unequivocally: "It was not the economists who liberated the slaves or who passed the Factory Acts, but the rash and ignorant Christians."[4]

Evangelism and Revolution

The first task for Wesley was always evangelism, not reform. Yet, in a century of striking contrast between excessive wealth and life-robbing poverty, Wesley raised the consciousness of a nation to a host of concerns, and to many of these hurts he brought relief and often basic reform.

His method was that of the evangelist. He appealed mainly for individual change and initiative in correcting social abuses. A socially sensitized will produced by an intense religious experience was the basis for his social strategy.

In this concern for personal change, Wesley managed to avoid the negativism and moralism so characteristic of many moral crusades. His stress was on the positive ideal of planting holiness in the hearts of men and women. His reform efforts also had a positive thrust due to his concern that a genuine "love of neighbor" (which always produces humility) not be lost in moral crusading.

There are times, as we shall see, when Wesley

appeals for change in unjust structures or calls for changes in government policy for a positive social result, but these are not common. In this sense, he was a conservative reformer, but an effective agent of real social change nonetheless. While he was not in the pattern of later Christian reformers, it is amazing how quickly Wesley was to perceive some of the social plagues of his time for what they were, how vigorously he denounced them, and how insistently he urged Methodists to avoid participation in them.[5]

Thus Wesley was, in Outler's words, "as much of an atypical revolutionary as he was an atypical evangelist." But his movement provided thousands of formerly faceless men and women with new experiences of personal dignity conferred on them by God. This created a social and political force in England that played a crucial role in what Wilberforce called "the revolution of manners and morals" in English society.[6]

Seven Areas of Mission

Let's look at a few examples of social responsibility from the Wesleyan Revival.

The poor. Wesley's own personal example must have been an inspiration to the early Methodists. Believing that money is a good servant but a bad master, Wesley chose to use his own money to serve others. He literally gave away most of his income through the years. He also gave himself in personal concern and risk.

Even past the age of eighty he spent five consecutive days in the middle of winter walking the streets of London from morning till evening ankle-deep in melting snow raising about a thousand dollars "to clothe them that needed it most." Outler knows of no other person in Wesley's century who so identified himself with the English poor or whose identification was more heartily accepted by them.

The early societies were involved in a host of ministries. There were literacy classes and a school for the poor which operated eleven hours a day. A medical clinic and drug dispensary met the health needs of the poor. Room and board were provided for destitute widows, orphans, and the blind. Self-help was encouraged through cottage industries and a credit union.

Poverty for Wesley was the misuse of community resources, the use of property with little or no social consideration. This grew out of his theological understanding of God as owner and persons as stewards. Irresponsible use of resources, particularly wasteful spending on luxuries by the wealthy, was the cause of much of the deprivation he saw. At times he even called for government action to relieve scarcity and hardship for the poor.

In all of this, there was no condescension toward the poor. Services were not withheld from any segment of the community in need, but, following

Wesley's admonition, special care was given to society members experiencing hardship. Few early Methodists were recipients of public relief because of their care for one another.

The *London Spectator* was so impressed, the following once appeared in its pages: "The Roman church has been called the church of the poor; but that title of honor belongs quite as much, if not with a better right, to the Wesleyan body." A contemporary commentator has put it this way: "When the poor gathered in huge throngs to hear Wesley preach, the ruling classes said he was threatening the social order. Indeed he was, not because he had a political message, but just because he treated the lower classes as human."[7]

Slavery. Wesley used the sharpest words in his vigorous attack on slavery. Rejecting the economic necessity of slavery, he further maintained that any wealth derived from human bondage was an affront to God. "Better is honest poverty," he wrote, "than all the riches brought in by tears, sweat and blood of our fellow creatures."[8] Although not all Methodists shared Wesley's passion, a large number actively engaged in the slavery struggle.

The last letter Wesley ever wrote, and one of the noblest, was the famous one presumed to have been addressed to William Wilberforce, in which he laid his hands in blessing, as it were, on the man who was to lead the anti-slavery fight in England to a successful conclusion. It contained these words: "Go on, in the name of God and in the power of His might, till even American slavery (the vilest that ever saw the sun) shall vanish away before it."[9]

Prisons. It is interesting to note in Christian history how often periods of renewal are characterized by concern for prisoners. John Wesley was acquainted with the conditions of his day, having preached in jails since his student days at Oxford. He also knew the injustices of the criminal justice system, particularly toward the poor, and the severity of punishment.

His call for ministry to those "fast bound in misery and iron" was sparked by scenes such as the one he describes after a trip to see prisoners near Bristol. "About eleven hundred of them . . . were confined in that little place without anything to lie on but a little dirty straw . . . so that they died like rotten sheep. I was much affected." He goes on to tell about raising money for clothes, blankets, and mattresses, "so that I believe from this time they were pretty well provided with all the necessaries of life."[10]

Liquor. Second only to his stand against the slave trade was Wesley's crusade against the sale and use of liquor. He opposed the liquor trade on social, humanitarian, and religious grounds. Liquor, which was consumed generously and without restraint in Wesley's day, robbed grain that could feed the poor, took away money needed for other purposes, destroyed the mind and body, and was a sin against God. For these reasons Wesley urged Methodists not to sell or drink liquor, and the General Rules forbade "drunkenness, buying or selling spirituous liquors;

or drinking them (unless in cases of extreme necessity)."

Politics. As quick as Wesley was to claim that he was a religious leader, not a politician, so was he to speak on affairs of state. His political impact was always significant through pamphlets, tracts, and sermons.

A conservative Tory by nature and nurture, his sympathies were on the side of the Crown and Constitution. The limited monarchy was his ideal. He had a reverential attitude toward social order and civil authority. It is strange that someone so close to the hopes and aspirations of the common people would so repudiate their involvement in governmental decision making. Wesley had no time for the idea that the people constitute the source of power in government.

He reprimanded the American colonies for severing the "sacred ties" that bound them to England. While initially supportive of the colonists, Wesley quickly changed his attitude at the prospect of violent revolution. Relations between American and British Methodists were severely strained because of Wesley's position.

Many scholars have noted that the ultimate effect of the Wesleyan Revival was far different from Wesley's political philosophy. People who had been given no significance by society heard a message of human dignity, worth, and freedom. They would never be the same again! Also, leadership opportunities were theirs for the first time through their participation in the societies and as lay preachers. Such experience was to serve them well as they moved into the political arena.

War. For Wesley war could be a legitimate activity of the state, but his predominant attitude was one of peace. "I am persuaded love and tender measures will do far more than violence."[11] Early Methodists were called to be active peacemakers, not just in the sense of preventing "this fire of hell from being kindled," but also "when it is kindled, from breaking out, or when it is broke out, from spreading any farther."[12]

While Wesley did not talk in terms of "just" and "unjust" wars, one can only assume that he would not have sanctioned an aggressive or "preventable" war. It appears that he would not sanction Christian participation in a war unless the war itself could be sanctioned. However, it is possible that he might have rationalized such participation, believing that Christians were putting an end to a war already under way.

Wesley's politics greatly influenced his thoughts on war: The soldier was viewed as a servant of both the king and God. Roland H. Bainton has pointed out that "the Anglicans were frequently Tories out of devotion to the king, the head not only of the state but also of the Church. The Methodists, only just emerging as a body separate from the Church of England, shared the same political outlook."[13]

Education. A concern for education emerged quickly in the Wesleyan Revival. John Wesley, whose own education began with instruction from his mother, felt that preachers and laity needed to be literate if they were to be reliable and responsible citizens. Schools for elementary instruction, dissemination of secular and religious literature, and the Sunday School movement represented significant educational efforts during the Wesleyan Revival.

A Personal and Social Reformation

In addition to acknowledging the social achievements of the Wesleyan Revival, this survey also exposes some of the serious weaknesses of Wesley's brand of social holiness. There is an authoritarianism and almost unquestioning loyalty in his political ethic. A pervasive individualism makes it hard for him to place some issues in their necessary social and systemic context. His concern for prisoners puts contemporary Christians to shame, but he does not question the unjust criminal justice system that put them there in the first place.

Yet, despite all the shortcomings, the Wesleyan Revival produced social reform of massive proportions. The spirit of revival sparked fires of change that could never have been predicted (nor condoned in many cases) by Wesley. Outler believes that Halvey's famous comment that Methodism saved England from the French Revolution misses the point—that the Wesleyan Revival actually sponsored a very different kind of revolution, an actual transformation of the social morals and manners of a nation.

Thus a conservative evangelist loosed a powerful agency for social change. Out of the Wesleyan Revival emerged a new class of men and women who provided the leadership muscle for a whole succession of social reforms, including the trade union movement, prison reform, and the abolition of slavery.[14]

Outler finds part of the secret in Wesley himself, not in his political or social theories, but in his "visible martyrdom and servanthood that rammed home the *evangelion* he preached. He taught his Methodists to be martyrs and servants." Outler continues with a good lesson in evangelism and social ethics: "The world hears the gospel when it sees it—when its witnesses are clearly concerned with human existence and clearly committed to a more fully human future, in this world and the next."[15]

The Wesleyan Revival consistently held together personal and social holiness. Such a witness can help guide all of us to a whole understanding of the gospel, whether we are more inclined to accommodate on personal ethics while challenging social evils or accommodate on social issues while maintaining admirable personal standards.

An older pastor wrote me recently after reading an article of mine on Christians and politics. After recounting his own personal involvements with controversial social issues and the attendant pain and misunderstanding, he wrote, "The gospel is personal first and social always. We can't separate the two."

When we are true to the heritage of the Wesleyan Revival, vital and life-changing religious experience is found side-by-side with vigorous and unrelenting social righteousness.

Questions for Thought and Discussion

1. For Wesley, social reform was rooted in a prior mission: personal evangelism. What do you believe is the relationship of reform and evangelism needed today?

2. "Irresponsible use of resources," "wasteful spending on luxuries"—how contemporary Wesley's economic concerns sound! Yet how simplistic (and effective) is the answer: his identification with the poor and his individual example. How could your response to poverty demonstrate such personal and relational witness more clearly?

3. You might profit from taking a current social problem—refugees, hunger, abused spouses, drug traffic—and imagining how Wesley would respond.

4. In approaching social ills today, how can we combine the personal servanthood of a Wesley with the needed reformation of complex causes?

CHRISTIAN STEWARDSHIP

John Wesley was always clear that money is an excellent gift of God. He was careful to insist that it is the love of money, not money itself, which is the root of all evil. Yet Wesley became deeply concerned as he saw Methodists, "with few exceptions", growing wealthier and at the same time decreasing in grace as they increased in wealth.

To those early Methodists Wesley implored: "The Lord of all will . . . inquire, 'How didst thou employ the worldly goods which I lodged in thy hands . . .? In what manner didst thou employ that comprehensive talent, money?' [By] first supplying thy own reasonable wants, together with those of the family; then restoring the remainder to me, through the poor, whom I had appointed to receive it.'"[1]

Wesley formulated this philosophy of giving in the following terms: "What way then . . . can we take that our money may not sink us to the nethermost hell? There is one way, and there is no other under heaven. If those who 'gain all they can' and 'save all they can' will likewise 'give all they can' then, the more they gain the more they will grow in grace, and the more treasure they will lay up in heaven.'"[2]

While most of us know the outline of Wesley's philosophy (gain, save, and give), we may only know it as a stereotype. Let's examine it more closely.

Gain All You Can

Could there be any more needless advice than this? The god of today's world is money. If there actually is an American religion, a value commitment that serves as the single unifying force within the nation, then it is money. Ernest Campbell is on target in describing acquisitiveness as a sin in very good standing today.

There is no denying that John Wesley did stress the pursuit of gain by honest industry, diligence, hard work, and initiative. However, the overwhelming emphasis in Wesley's discussion of "gain all you can" was not the pursuit of wealth so much as restrictions on the pursuit of wealth. Wesley's discussion can in no way be viewed as cheerleading for unbridled acquisition.

Wesley said that money is not to be made at the expense of life, at the expense of health (which for Wesley was the same thing), or at the expense of hurting the mind. Nor was it to be made in ways that would hurt one's neighbor financially (through overcharging or high interest rates), or bodily (Wesley used this as an opportunity to condemn "liquid fire" and the "poisoners general" who deal in this commodity), or spiritually.

There may be an important word here for those of us who so casually ignore the human trade-offs that are a part of American prosperity. Wesley was not quite so blind.

Save All You Can

A man once said to me, "One of the significant factors in my accumulated wealth is that I have always followed John Wesley's philosophy of saving all you can. Even in the days when I made a meager income," he continued, "I always put a little of that money away in a savings account."

Wesley was not talking about that kind of saving when he said to save all you can. Putting money in a bank was the furthest thing from his mind. What he meant was refraining from needless spending.

He noted with indignation the waste in the houses of the wealthy, which he regarded as one of the significant causes of poverty in his day. As he put it, "Only look into the kitchens of the great, the nobility and the gentry, almost without exception, and when you have observed the amazing waste which is made there you will no longer wonder at the scarcity."[3]

And so, Wesley said, we are to avoid unnecessary spending on such matters as these:

—Do not spend money to gratify the desires of the flesh. He said, "Be content with what plain nature requires."

—Do not spend money to gratify the desires of the eye. He referred here to expensive apparel, needless ornaments, expensive furniture, etc. He said, "Let your neighbors buy those things—your neighbors who don't know any better than to do this kind of thing."

—Do not spend money to gain admiration or praise. Don't buy applause.

—Do not throw away money on your children in delicate food or costly apparel. "Why should you purchase for them more pride, vanity, etc.?" said Wesley. "They don't want anymore; they have enough already."

—And do not save money to leave to your children so they can throw it away.[4]

Here, again, is a word for us, living with our tremendous obsession with self. An entire period becomes known as the "Me Decade." Our best sellers talk about "Looking Out for Number One" and "Pulling Your Own Strings." Our commercials tell us, "You owe it to yourself" and "It costs more, but I'm worth it."

We give lip service to what John Wesley was talking about because it's the thing to do. We have brought together in a strange combination an obsession with self and a verbal commitment to sacrifice.

So we lament world hunger, and we genuinely do want to feel that we as a church and as a nation are responding to the world's overwhelming need for food. But at the same time 25 percent of the food that is consumed in the United States is used to achieve or maintain overweight.

Maybe a lot of us are saying that we are willing to

accept any sacrifice, just so long as it is somebody else who does the sacrificing. We can live with any change of lifestyle, so long as it does not bother *our* lifestyle.

Wesley has a word to a people preoccupied with consumption. While the slogan, "Live simply that others may simply live" is new, the intent is old in the Wesleyan heritage.

Give All You Can

When John Wesley said give all you can, he meant *all*. "I do not say, 'Be a good Jew, giving a tenth of all you possess,' I do not say, 'Be a good Pharisee, giving a fifth of all your substance,' I dare not advise you to give half of what you have; no, nor three-quarters, but all."[5]

Wesley did not ask us to "give all you *can*." His emphasis was closer to "Give *all*; you can!"

Wesley followed his own advice. As a student he learned that he could live on a certain amount each week. As his income increased through the years, he continued to live on the same amount and give away the rest. His record shows that one year he received 30 pounds, lived on 28 pounds and gave away 2 pounds. The second year he received 60 pounds, lived on 28 pounds and gave away 32 pounds. The third year he received 90 pounds, lived on 28 pounds and gave away 62. The fourth year he received 120 pounds, lived on 28 pounds and gave away 92.

He told his sister: "Money never stays with me. It would burn me if it did. I throw it out of my hands as soon as possible, lest it should find its way into my heart." He told everyone that, if at his death he had more than ten pounds in his possession, people had the privilege of calling him a robber. The history of philanthropy by Wesley and the early Methodists is extensive and generally well known.

Here is found the heart of Wesley's philosophy of giving; without it the other parts have no meaning. Yet, it is precisely here that the limitations of his stewardship philosophy become quite apparent: for example, the individualism and the naive economic assumptions.

Through Wesley's approach God's care became real for persons. His giving demonstrated genuine care for people. Lives were transformed and liberated through it. Human dignity was protected by not treating people as if they existed for the sake of philanthropy.

Some say that the most socially revolutionary aspect of the Wesleyan Revival was the sense of worth, dignity, and personality that people came to have. The early Methodists gave more than money, food, and medicine. They gave themselves, their love, their care. They gave Christ in a living and vital way. To confuse Wesleyan giving with condescending handouts is to ignore the testimony of that era.

Bridging the Gap

History has shown that Wesley had every reason to be concerned with what was happening to Methodists as they became more prosperous and moved out of the lowest social classes. Social historians have now documented what Wesley was beginning to feel—that "rising prosperity of the Methodists (particularly those of the Wesleyan connection) cut them off from the close sympathy with working" people.[6]

Some of the most haunting words that I have come across are by C. Eric Lincoln: "You will work for them but not with them. Your heart will bleed for them but not your head or your hands. You will be their advocate but not their friend. You will sponsor them and their causes, but their cause is not your cause anymore because you are middle class."[7]

That is a gap which cannot be bridged by ideas or doctrines but only by a changed heart and soul and mind to go with whatever stewardship philosophy we have. The testimony of the Wesleyan Revival is that the gap was bridged in a significant way and that it can be bridged in any time by God's faithful people.

Questions for Thought and Discussion

1. How do you interpret Wesley's "Gain all you can"? In today's world what sort of restraints on our earning would Wesley urge?

2. What does "Save all you can" mean to you? Our new awareness of limited resources in a hungry world gives Wesley's charge some new connotations. Try rephrasing his five "Do nots" (p. 47) for our time.

3. How do you respond to Wesley's own simple lifestyle and refusal to accumulate any wealth? How do you apply his "Give all you can" to your own stewardship?

Conclusion
The Legacy of the
Wesleyan Revival

What, then, are the chief theological characteristics of the Wesleyan Revival? What are the overall features that stand out?

A Theology of Balance

First, the theology at the heart of the Wesleyan Revival was a *theology of balance*.

Bishop Stokes calls it Christianity with "vital balance." This balance is found over and over in Wesleyan thought and practice.

It can be seen in the balance between theological freedom and doctrinal responsibility. People are free to believe as they are led to believe, but they are expected to believe in God's essential truths. We do not have a lot of doctrinal tests for membership, but we have essential doctrines that are the heart of our faith. On the one hand, we give great latitude in opinions and we do not expect everybody to be the same theologically, socially, politically, etc. But, on the other hand, we expect all to join together in the great cause of Jesus Christ as Lord and Savior. The Doctrinal Standards statement of The United Methodist Church rejects both doctrinal dogmatism and doctrinal indifferentism while commending the classic affirmation: "In essentials, unity; in non-essentials, liberty; and, in all things, charity."[1]

There is also a vital balance maintained between the practical and the doctrinal. Wesley's sermons dealt with practical matters of Christian living and also with doctrinal matters. Of the forty-four sermons in the collection which he gave to the public, twenty-four deal with practical concerns of Christian living, many being based on texts from the Sermon on the Mount. The other twenty deal with more abstract theological issues.[2]

One also finds a theology of balance in the way John Wesley treated the two competing doctrines of his day, the evangelical and the Catholic. While others were choosing sides, Wesley was the synthesizer who saw that these are not the only options. He developed what Outler calls a "third alternative" that brought together the concept of God's sovereignty (evangelical) with human responsibility (Catholic) into one system of theology. Wesley stressed *both* the Reformation emphasis on grace and the Roman Catholic emphasis on works. The way in which he held these two together represents the essence of this balance.

It is important to note that Wesley's balance is almost always a "both-and" kind of balance rather than a compromise between two extremes. George E. Koehler has outlined Wesley's balance in terms of these polarities:

Faith	Works
Gospel	Law
Scripture	Experience
Justification	Sanctification
Word	Sacraments
Criticism of church	Support of church

Of course, Wesley's formulation and use of the Quadrilateral (scripture, tradition, experience, and reason) represents a supreme example of the balance found throughout his theological method.

A Theology for People

The theology at the heart of the Wesleyan Revival was a *theology for people*.

Outler calls Wesley a "folk theologian," whom ordinary people heard gladly. He was a popularizer to whom the common people responded with uncommon enthusiasm. Although he was a man of training, sophistication, culture, and letters, he could talk to people in ways they heard and responded to, while others in his day were failing to reach them. He was a working theologian in the sense that his theology was worked out in the midst of the concerns and needs of real people in his day. He cared for people. His theology was always for people, and never placed people at the service of theology. It always served to illuminate their faith and to enable their salvation.

Notice how his texts tend to vary with the congregation to which he is preaching.

One day in 1742 he came into Newcastle, a center of the coal industry. He saw things there he had never seen before. He saw suffering, encountered low morality, and heard cursing by children and adults. He saw all of these things, but, basically, he saw a bruised people, a hurting people. They were a sinful people, to be sure, but a people in pain because the conditions of their economic life were stifling them and pulling them down.

When Sunday morning came, he went to the middle of the most evil part of Newcastle and started preaching with only one person standing by his side. He took for his text that day Isaiah 53:5: "He was wounded for our transgressions; he was bruised for our iniquities: the chastisement of our peace was upon him; and with his stripes we are healed." Before he got through preaching that morning, 1200 people had gathered around to hear him. More came back that evening.

But when he went to the church at Clifton filled with wealthy persons, his text was different: "I come not to call the righteous, but sinners to repentance" (Mark 2:17). Then on another occasion when he was preaching to a fashionable congregation he took as his text, "Ye serpents, ye generation of vipers, how can ye escape the damnation of hell?" (Matt. 23:33).

Some protested, but Wesley replied: "Oh, but if I were at Billingsgate (a much less affluent place) I would have taken, 'Behold the Lamb of God, which taketh away the sins of the world'" (John 1:29).[3]

He was a theologian who cared about people. He had the bias that the Bible has, the bias that God has had through history: for those on the bottom, for those most in need, for those hurting the most, for those suffering the most.

His quarrel, in his day, was not merely over the truthfulness of doctrine or beliefs. His quarrel was with doctrine that sets up shop for itself and is unrelated and unresponsive to people.

We need to hear that. When so many have narrow doctrinal tests for others, we need to hear John Wesley saying that people are not made for doctrines. Doctrine is a way of communicating the love of God to people in an understandable way that meets their needs.

He loved people. He had a concern for people and for their needs. He was a genuine folk theologian in that sense.

A Theology of Salvation

The theology at the heart of the Wesleyan Revival was above all else a *theology of salvation*.

Every sermon, every doctrine, every quotation revolves around this center—a theology of salvation. Wesley had a passion for humanity to come to know the joy of salvation, to know the grace that comes from God through Jesus Christ. This was his overriding preoccupation, his paramount concern.

This was at the heart of his entire life's work.

There is no way to understand anything Wesley said without first understanding his passion for a theology of salvation. His preaching was a preaching of salvation. His teaching was a teaching of salvation. His ethics were ethics that emerge from the experience of salvation. His understanding of stewardship evolved out of his theology of salvation.

The Episcopalian, Phillips Brooks, in his famous lectures to the divinity students at Yale, said, "Preach doctrine, preach all the doctrine that you know, and learn forever more and more; but preach it always, not that men may believe it, but that men may be saved by believing it."[4] That sums up very well what was at the heart of everything that John Wesley said and did.

The most important thing about Wesley and the leaders of the Wesleyan Revival is that they were persons of God, persons who knew God and knew how to lead others to the knowledge of God. Such knowledge, as Philip Watson has observed, is neither the product nor the property of any one century.[5] From such an example we can all learn.

Wesley's Embracing Vision

Phillips Brooks also tells of his first days in a divinity school. He had come from a college where the students studied hard but said nothing about faith. His first experience with a prayer meeting came at the seminary, and he was impressed with the devoutness of the participants. However, the next day in the Greek class he noted that some of the most devout students were unprepared in their lessons. Brooks commented that "the boiler had no connection with the engine."[6]

In the Wesleyan Revival, there was always a vital connection between boiler and engine, between spirit and mind, between message and action. Perhaps there is a loss of spiritual power today because we have cut ourselves off from the source of power. Perhaps we descendants of John Wesley have cut ourselves off from the message that energized the Wesleyan Revival.

We talk about Wesley's warmed heart but sometimes forget the fire that warmed it. In exhorting people to warmth, we need to remember that a person cannot generate his or her own heat. We must speak words aflame with the love of God in Christ, words which can kindle a fire.[7]

Albert C. Outler has spent a lifetime seeking to recover this Wesleyan message not only for his own denomination but also for the ecumenical world. From his study Outler finds back of and beyond Wesley's dated "opinions" a total view of the Christian life that is comprehensive and realistic. It is a view of God above all, and all else in and from God; of a human flaw that runs deeper than any human cure for it; of Christ's suffering love as the Father's redemptive love, restoring our lost humanity; of the Holy Spirit as God's inspiring presence. The hungers of the human heart cry out for such a powerful gospel. The church longs for such a theology which is truly catholic, truly evangelical and truly re-formed, all together.

Outler goes on to say that, like Simeon, he keeps looking toward a day when Wesley's embracing vision of God's grace bringing human nature to its full potential may find a rightful place in the kind of Christianity that will survive the crises that lie ahead.

"If I were a young man," Outler continues, "now in a time when the great systems have collapsed and the church's most desperate need is for a pastoral theology that understands and cares for Christ's flock, a working theology that is anchored in revelation and that swings wide and free to liberate people for the only freedom (in Christ) that will make them truly free, I think I'd explore John Wesley as a new frontier, with the same freedom to update him that he felt toward his own complex heritage."

"And, even in my own westering years," Outler concludes, "it still seems to be the best bet on the current theological tote-board."[8]

"The Best of All"

Even Wesley's death was a witness to that faith and message which had nourished and sustained him and the Wesleyan Revival. He spoke often of "holy living" and "holy dying." Truly, his death in 1791 at the age of eighty-eight was a holy experience.

CONCLUSION

Lying on his deathbed in a small room in the house on City Road, London, he astonished those present by breaking into the Isaac Watts hymn:

I'll praise my Maker while I've breath;
And when my voice is lost in death,
Praise shall employ my nobler powers.
My days of praise shall ne'er be past,
While life, and thought, and being last,
Or immortality endures.

He lived into the following day, summoning his little remaining strength for these final words: "The best of all is, God is with us."

He died, quietly, the following morning. May his message never die.

Questions for Thought and Discussion

1. Wesley's balanced theology has stood the test of time and led the people called Methodists around the world. Are there any ways it is getting "out of balance" today? For example, in your congregation is belief in God's sovereignty still in balance with belief in our human responsibility? What might you do to encourage a sound theological balance?

2. As you hear Christian doctrine taught and preached, is it carefully related to the needs of the people, as Wesley tried to do? How could this be done better? How can you do it as you share your beliefs with others?

3. Now that you have reviewed John Wesley's message, what aspects seem to have touched your life most directly through the years? What aspects hold promise for further exploration in your journey of faith?

NOTES

PREFACE

1. Stanley Ayling, *John Wesley* (Cleveland and New York: William Collins Publishers, 1979), p. 318.

INTRODUCTION: THEOLOGY AT THE HEART OF THE WESLEYAN REVIVAL

1. November 10, 1947.
2. Quoted in S. Paul Schilling, *Methodism and Society in Theological Perspective* (New York: Abingdon Press, 1960), p. 24.
3. "Doctrinal Standards in The United Methodist Church," *Perkins Journal*, Volume XXVIII, Number 1 (Fall 1974), 20.
4. *John Wesley's Theology Today* (Nashville: Abingdon, 1960), p. 5.
5. Thomas Jackson (ed.), *The Works of John Wesley, A. M.*, Third Edition (London: John Mason, 1829), VIII, 340. Hereafter cited as *Works*.
6. Edward H. Sugden (ed.), *Wesley's Standard Sermons*, Sixth Edition (London: Epworth Press, 1966), II, 522. Hereafter cited as *Sermons*.
7. Nehemiah Curnock (ed.), *The Journal of John Wesley*, Standard Edition (London: Epworth Press, 1938), VII, 389. Hereafter cited as *Journal*.
8. *Sermons*, II, 143.
9. Schilling, *Methodism and Society in Historical Perspective* (New York: Abingdon Press, 1961), p. 32.
10. *The Book of Discipline 1980*, (Nashville: United Method-

ist Publishing House), pp. 78-81. Hereafter cited as *Discipline*.

11. Quoted in Richard M. Cameron, *Methodism and Society in Historical Perspective* (New York: Abingdon Press, 1961), p. 32.

THE IMAGE OF GOD AND ORIGINAL SIN

1. *Sermons*, I, 116.
2. Ibid., II, 227-228.
3. *Works*, VI, 244.
4. *Works*, VI, 223.
5. *Works*, IX, 273.
6. *The Children of Light and the Children of Darkness* (New York: Charles Scribner's Sons, 1944), p. 16.
7. *Willson Lectures* (Washington: Wesley Theological Seminary, 1973), p. 15.

PREVENIENT GRACE AND REPENTANCE

1. *Works*, VI, 509.
2. *Works*, VI, 513.
3. *Sermons*, I, 155.
4. Quoted in Schilling, *Methodism and Society in Theological Perspective*, p. 63.
5. William Ragsdale Cannon, *The Theology of John Wesley* (New York: Abingdon - Cokesbury Press, 1946), pp. 109-117.

JUSTIFICATION BY FAITH

1. Cf. *Works*, VIII, 35; Robert E. Chiles, *Theological Transition in American Methodism: 1790-1935* (New York: Abingdon Press, 1965), p. 115; Albert C. Outler, *Theology in the Wesleyan Spirit* (Nashville: Discipleship Resources,

1975), p. 54; and Mack B. Stokes, *Our Methodist Heritage* (Nashville: Graded Press, 1963), p. 42.

2. The summary in this section is that of Williams, *John Wesley's Theology Today*, p. 75.

3. *Theology in the Wesleyan Spirit*, p. 45.

4. *Sermons*, I, 47.

5. Schilling, *Methodism and Society in Theological Perspective*, pp. 49-50. Cf. *Works*, VII, 375-383.

6. Chiles, *Theological Transition in American Methodism: 1790-1935*, p. 157.

7. Cf. Williams, *John Wesley's Theology Today*, pp. 69-71.

8. *Works*, VI, 527.

9. Cf. Schilling, *Methodism and Society in Theological Perspective*, p. 222.

THE WITNESS OF THE SPIRIT

1. *Sermons*, II, 343-344.

2. Ibid., 357.

3. Ibid., I, 201.

4. Ibid., 200.

5. Quoted in Schilling, *Methodism and Society in Theological Perspective*, p. 53.

6. Williams, *John Wesley's Theology Today*, pp. 108-110.

7. *Sermons*, II, 358.

THE CHURCH AND THE CHRISTIAN LIFE

1. *Discipline*, 1980, p. 58.

2. *Works*, VIII, 31.

3. *Sermons*, I, 242.

4. *Sermons*, I, 259-260.

5. *Works*, I, 278f.; *Sermons*, I, 245-248.

6. *Works*, V, 193; *Sermons*, I, 248-251.

7. *Works*, I, 279f.; *Sermons*, I, 251-253. Albert Outler reminds me that this statement is misleading in modern

ecclesiological terms. Wesley was assuming that the "believers" about whom he was talking were at least baptized and (most of them) confirmed. Thus, the distinction between "converting" and "confirming" meant something very different to him and to his hearers than to people who have had no religious upbringing.
8. *Works*, V, 345-60.

GROWTH THROUGH CHRISTIAN COMMUNITY

1. Outler, "Pastoral Care in the Wesleyan Spirit," *Perkins Journal*, XXVI, 1 (Fall 1971), 5.
2. *Journal*, V, 26.
3. Williams, *John Wesley's Theology Today*, p. 151.
4. Ibid., pp. 150-152.
5. Outler, "Pastoral Care in the Wesleyan Spirit," 5-6.
6. Albert C. Outler (ed.), *John Wesley* (New York: Oxford University Press, 1964), pp. 180-181.
7. *Works*, VIII, 270-271.

HOLINESS OF HEART AND LIFE

1. Roy H. Short, *History of the Council of Bishops of The United Methodist Church* (Nashville: Abingdon, 1980), pp. 62-63.
2. Ayling, *John Wesley*, p. 210.
3. *Sermons*, II, 150-151.
4. *Works*, XII, 241.
5. J. Russell Hale, *The Unchurched* (New York: Harper & Row, 1980), p. 188.
6. Quoted in Outler, *Willson Lectures*, p. 16.
7. *Works*, IX, 235.
8. John Telford (ed.), *The Letters of John Wesley*, Standard Edition (London: Epworth Press, 1931), VIII, 238. Hereafter cited as *Letters*.
9. *Theological Transition in American Methodism: 1790-1935*, p. 30.
10. *Theology in the Wesleyan Spirit*, p. 39. Outler adds that

all the Reformers taught some sort of linkage. But in Wesley one finds a special type that normally involved four steps (repentance, justification, regeneration, sanctification) and a certain sort of life-process between justification and sanctification. Thus, justification is more of a *state* (a new relation between God and persons of pardon and reconciliation) whereas holy living and its end, sanctification, are more of a *process*, involving time and the Christian experience of assurance.

11. "The New Sanctification," *Methodist Review*, 94 (1912), 80. Quoted in Schilling, *Methodism and Society in Theological Perspective*, p. 78.

12. Cf. Theodore H. Runyon, *Sanctification and Liberation: A Reexamination in the Light of the Wesleyan Tradition* (Nashville: Abingdon, 1981).

SOCIAL HOLINESS

1. Dag Hammarskjöld, *Markings* (New York: Alfred A Knopf, 1964), p. 122.

2. *Works*, V, 296.

3. John Emory (ed.), *The Works of the Reverend John Wesley, A.M.* (New York: 1831), VII, 593. Hereafter cited as *Works* (Emory).

4. Quoted in Schilling, *Methodism and Society in Theological Perspective*, p. 64.

5. Cameron, *Methodism and Society in Historical Perspective*, p. 50.

6. Outler, *Willson Lectures*, p. 4.

7. George F. Will, "The Subversive Pope," *Newsweek*, October 15, 1979, p. 140.

8. *Works*, XI, 74.

9. Quoted in Cameron, *Methodism and Society in Historical Perspective*, p. 53.

10. Quoted Ibid., p. 48.

11. *Letters*, II, 361.

12. *Works* (Emory), 203.

13. Roland H. Bainton, *Christian Attitudes Toward War and Peace* (New York: Abingdon Press, 1960), p. 189.
14. Outler, *Evangelism in the Wesleyan Spirit* (Nashville: Tidings, 1971), pp. 30-31.
15. Ibid., pp. 103, 104.

CHRISTIAN STEWARDSHIP

1. *Works*, I, 455-456.
2. *Works*, VII, 317.
3. *Works*, VI, 274, 275-276.
4. *Sermons*, II, 320-323.
5. *Works*, VII, 9-10.
6. Cameron, *Methodism and Society in Historical Perspective*, p. 73.
7. Quoted in Frederick Herzog, "United Methodism in Agony?" *Perkins Journal*, Volume XXVIII, Number 1 (Fall 1974), 1.

CONCLUSION: THE LEGACY OF THE WESLEYAN REVIVAL

1. *Discipline*, 1980, p. 73.
2. Halford E. Luccock et al., *The Story of Methodism* (New York: Abingdon Press, 1949), p. 97.
3. Ibid., p. 99.
4. Schilling, *Methodism and Society in Theological Perspective*, p. 42.
5. Philip S. Watson, *The Message of the Wesleys: A Reader of Instruction and Devotion* (New York: Macmillan Company, 1964), p. xv.
6. *Phillips Brooks on Preaching* (New York: Seabury Press, 1964), p. 44, quoted in Ronald E. Sleeth, *Which Way to God?* (Nashville: Abingdon, 1968), p. 65.
7. Watson, *The Message of the Wesleys*, p. 8.
8. Outler, *Willson Lectures*, pp. 7, 8, 9, 19. *Evangelism in the Wesleyan Spirit*, p. 55.